MR. TEST

by Paul Eldridge

For Roger - thank you for the fun.

And for big kids who should know better.

This is the delightful tale of Mr Testy.

Today Mr Testy is visiting Jollytown. Mr Testy doesn't really like Jollytown.

That's because most of the time Mr Testy is an angry little bastard.

As Mr Testy walks through Jollytown, some of the local townsfolk start to point at Mr Testy.

And then they start to laugh at him.

This makes Mr Testy ever so slightly... well, testy.

Mr Testy walks over to the townsfolk, raises his mighty weapon high above his head and says...

"Mock me and I shall smite thee!".

Much to Mr Testy's surprise the townsfolk continue to point, and then begin to laugh even harder.

This makes Mr Testy very angry.

So Mr Testy decides to teach these cheeky twats a lesson...

And kicks them all soundly in the testicles!

"Oh hello there, what's going on here then?" says a voice.

Mr Testy turns around to see the Bishop of Jollytown, he seems rather interested in the kicking that Mr Testy is administering to the townsfolk.

"Ha ha ha." starts to laugh the bishop, as he too begins to point at Mr Testy.

"Look at the state of you." he says, "You're like a big hairy nut."

Mr Testy finds this inappropriate behaviour from a member of the clergy rather irksome.

Mr Testy snatches the bishop's crook from him and tells the bishop that he should not mock him, or he will smite him such as his lord would do.

The bishop continues to point and laugh with even more vigour. So Mr Testy proceeds to bash the bishop. And not just once, he bashes the bishop again and again and again and again.

Mr Testy continues to bash the bishop until a throbbing purple lump rises all the way to the top of his silly hat.
"Bad bishop." says Mr Testy, "Bad bad bad bishop."

Mr Testy decides to walk on further into Jollytown, even though he is beginning to think that the populace are actually rather insulting and not just playing silly buggers.

Suddenly Mr Testy hears a lady scream, "Help help." she screams.

The lady runs around with her arms in the air, "He's grabbing my melons." she screams, as a naughty monkey grasps a pair of the firm watery fruit from her fruits and vegetables market stall.

"Ooh ooh ooh." laughs the monkey as he begins jerking on a gherkin.

Mr Testy finds that this naughty monkey's rude behaviour vexes him greatly. The monkey is very fast and tries to run away with his loot, but he's not faster than a vexed Mr Testy, who grabs the naughty monkey firmly in both hands and bends him over his knee.

"Naughty monkey." says Mr Testy, "Naughty naughty monkey." he says, as he spanks the monkey so hard that his bottom becomes bright red and very sore indeed.

"Yes." says the lady excitedly, "Spank that monkey." she says with glee, "Faster, faster, faster, spank him hard." she screams with a saucy glint in her eye.

"Thank you." says the lady as Mr Testy releases the punished primate, "Now if only you could handle the farmer's cock for me." she adds.

"It keeps me up at night and gives me no rest whatsoever." she continues to say as Mr Testy begins to become a little dismayed.

"It crows all day and all night long, not just in the morning." says the lady, much to Mr Testy's relief.

Thinking that maybe the lady will put out, Mr Testy goes to see the farmer and asks him if he can keep his cock quiet.

The farmer points and laughs at Mr Testy just like the other townsfolk did.

So Mr Testy punches him in the face and smacks his bitch-ass fat farmer's butt to the curb.

The farmer's cock is not hard for Mr Testy to find, because he is constantly crowing and Mr Testy realises that the lady was right, it is really really clucking annoying.

Mr Testy grabs the farmer's cock around its scrawny squarking neck, and with a nice firm grip he chokes that chicken, chokes him hard, shutting that little shit up good and proper.

The lady says thank you to Mr Testy, but doesn't give him any, Mr Testy takes umbrage at this and storms off shouting some very naughty words.

Mr Testy has really had enough of Jollytown now and feels like leaving.

As he walks to the road out of town, more of the townsfolk point and laugh at Mr Testy, which perturbs him somewhat more.

After bashing the bishop, spanking the monkey and choking the chicken, Mr Testy thinks this lot really are taking the piss.

So Mr Testy decides that maybe he will not leave Jollytown quite just yet, and he turns to address the mocking townsfolk.

"Shut the fuck up you fucking piss taking bunch of fucking fuckers!"
exclaims Mr Testy, using some rather inappropriate language for a children's book.

What Mr Testy really wants to do, he thinks to himself, is give this lot of ungrateful fucking wankers a damn good kicking.

And do you know what Mr Testy did then?..
He firmly grasped his mighty weapon,
flexed his toes in his best kicking boots...

and began to smile.

Also Available

MR. TESTY
COLOURING BOOK
by Paul Eldridge

A Gonad The Barbarian Adventure

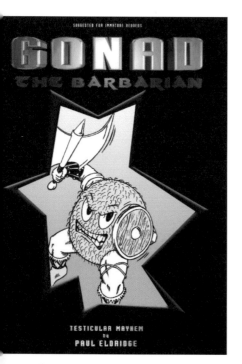

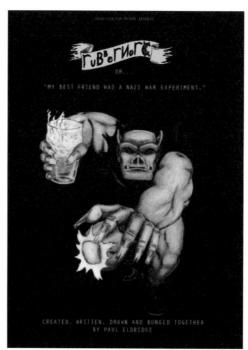

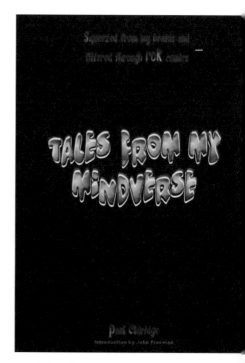

Gonad The Barbarian

Rubbernorc

Tales From My Mindverse

25980601R00020

Printed in Great Britain
by Amazon